THE EARLY RISHONIM

A Gemara Student's Guide

Copyright © 2015 by Aryeh J. Leibowitz

Updated Edition 2.2 (11/2021)

All Rights Reserved

No part of this publication may be translated, reproduced, stored in a retrieval system, or transmitted in any form or by any means, electronic, mechanical, photocopying, recording, or otherwise, without prior permission in writing from the copyright holder.

ISBN-13: 978-1515168447

ISBN-10: 1515168441

Comments, questions, or corrections are welcome:
Ajleibow@gmail.com

TABLE OF CONTENTS

PREFACE 5
INTRODUCTION 7

THE EARLY RISHONIM OF NORTH AFRICA 11
General Historical Overview 12
R. Yaakov and R. Nisim of Kairouan 14
R. Chananel b. Chushiel (רבינו חננאל) 15
R. Yitzchak Alfasi (רי״ף) 16
The End of the Early Rishonim in N. Africa 20

THE EARLY RISHONIM OF SOUTHERN SPAIN 21
General Historical Overview 22
R. Shmuel HaNagid (ר׳ שמואל הנגיד) 23
R. Yitzchak Ibn Gayas (רי״ץ גיות) 24
R. Yosef ibn Migash (רי״י מיגאש) 25
R. Moshe b. Maimon (רמב״ם) 27
The End of the Early Rishonim in Spain 32

THE EARLY RISHONIM OF ASHKENAZ 35
General Historical Overview 36
Rabbenu Gershom (רבינו גרשום) 37
The German Yeshivos 38
R. Shlomo b. Yitzchak (רש״י) 39

The Crusades 42
The Ba'alei Tosafos (בעלי תוספות) 43
R. Shmuel b. Meir (רשב״ם) 47
R. Yaakov b. Meir (רבינו תם) 47
R. Tam's Contemporaries and Students 49
R. Yitzchak b. Shmuel (ר״י הזקן) 51
Talmidei HaRi 53
The Talmudists of Germany 57
R. Eliezer b. Nosson (ראב״ן) 57
Chasidei Ashkenaz 58
Students of the Raavan 60
R. Eliezer b. Yoel HaLevi (ראבי״ה) 60
The Ravyah's Contemporaries 61

THE EARLY RISHONIM OF PROVENCE 65
The Torah Community of Catalonia 66
General Historical Overview 67
R. Avraham B. Yitzchak (רב אב ב״ד) 67
R. Zerachiah HaLevi (בעל המאור/רז״ה) 68
R. Yitchak b. Abba Mari of Marseilles (בעל העיטור) . 69
R. Avraham b. Dovid (ראב״ד) 70
R. Yonason of Lunel (ר״י מלוניל) 71

EPILOGUE 75

PREFACE

STUDENTS OF *GEMARA* merit to spend hours analyzing the words of our holy ancestors, the *Rishonim*. But who were the *Rishonim*? When did they live? Who were their teachers? What was unique about their *seforim*, or their *derech halimud*? The goal of this short pamphlet is to address these questions.

This pamphlet is not written as a history book, nor is its goal to simply teach "history." It does not dwell on dates (many of those that appear are approximations), or historical events. Rather, this pamphlet presents the major streams of transmission of the *masorah* following the demise of the Babylonian *yeshivos* under the *Geonim*. Its focus is primarily on the study of *Gemara*, and does not address the major contributions of many *Rishonim* in other fields, such as Jewish thought and *Tanach*.

◊ ◊ ◊

I wish to thank a number of *talmidim* that assisted with the editing and proofreading of this pamphlet. Mordechai Djavaheri, Micah Hyman, and Nachi Penn all volunteered their time to read through the pamphlet, and they all made excellent *he'aros* that greatly enhanced the final product. I also thank my parents for reviewing this pamphlet and for all their advice, and I thank my wife for all her encouragement and support.

Several works were helpful in preparing this pamphlet. I would like to specifically acknowledge the published works of Ephraim Urbach and Yisrael Tashma. I would also like to acknowledge the scholarship of Rabbis Elazar Hurvitz, Ephraim Kanarfogel, Haym Soloveitchik and Shlomo Toledano.

It is my hope that this pamphlet will engender in its readers a true appreciation for the *chachmei hamesorah*, and inspire them to increase their dedication to *limud haTorah*, as they see with greater clarity that we today are another link in the illustrious chain of transmission that has sustained and inspired our nation throughout the millennia.

Sha'alvim, Israel
7 Av, 5775

INTRODUCTION

Ever since the Torah was given to the people of Israel at Sinai, the transmission, interpretation, and safeguarding of the Torah was in the hands of the generation's greatest scholars. Throughout biblical history, each generation looked to the *Beis Din HaGadol*, also known as the Sanhedrin, for Torah leadership. This body of leading scholars was led by the *Nasi* (President) and *Av Beis Din* (Chief Justice) as the Sanhedrin taught the Torah, interpreted its laws, adjudicated cases, and enacted *takanos* and *gezeiros*. The Sanhedrin was also uniquely empowered to appoint kings, annex new sections of Jerusalem, and carry out other national functions. Additionally, the Sanhedrin judged capital cases, sanctified the new moon, and were responsible for a host of other duties.[1]

Moshe Rabbenu was the first to preside over the *Beis Din HaGadol*. After him, this role was passed on to his student Yehoshua, and so it continued through the generations. Shmuel, Eliyahu, Yeshayahu, Yirmiyahu – to name just a few links in the chain of the *masorah* – all presided over the

---

[1] See the Rambam's *Mishna Torah Hilchos Sanhedrin* 5 and *Hilchos Melachim* 1:3.

Sanhedrin and were the Torah leaders of their respective generations.[2]

With the destruction of the *Beis HaMikdash*, the Sanhedrin was exiled to Bavel, where it was presided over by great scholars, such as Yechezkel and Baruch Ben Neriah.[3] With the return from the Babylonian exile, the Sanhedrin began to operate again in Israel.

During the early years of the second *Beis HaMikdash* period, Ezra presided over the Sanhedrin and instituted many important enactments. Due to the important work of his Sanhedrin, it became known as the *Anshei Keneses HaGedolah*, and its members included some of the last prophets.[4] The Sanhedrin maintained Torah leadership and

---

[2] See the Rambam's introduction to *Mishna Torah* for a complete list of the transmission of Torah through the generations. It would appear that not all those listed were officially on the Sanhedrin, for kings were not allowed to be members of the Sanhedrin (Rambam, *Hilchos Sanhedrin* 1:4-5).

[3] Jews lived mostly in Israel during the time period of Jewish monarchy, but they began to arrive in *Bavel* as a result of the Assyrian (אשור) conquest of the Northern Kingdom of Israel. The next major migration to *Bavel* came over a hundred years later when Yehoyachin, King of Yehuda, was exiled to *Bavel*. Another wave followed after the destruction of the first *Beis HaMikdash*. However, not all Jews fled to *Bavel*, as we find communities emerging in other neighboring regions, such as Alexandria, Egypt. A few decades later, many Jews from *Bavel* – led in part by Nechemiah and Ezra – returned to Israel to rebuild the *Beis HaMikdash*. However, others chose to remain in exile.

[4] See *Yoma* 69b and the Rambam's introduction to *Mishna Torah*.

continued to be active even after the Romans destroyed the second *Beis HaMikdash*.

After the destruction of the second *Beis HaMikdash*, many Jews fled the land of Israel and moved to *Bavel*. Others were forcibly exiled throughout the Roman Empire. The result was that small Jewish communities began to appear in Europe and North Africa.[5] Nonetheless, the center of Jewish learning remained in Israel, and revolved around the *Tanaaim*, many of whom were members of the Sanhedrin. Their Torah scholarship was codified into the *Mishna* by R. Yehuda HaNasi around the year 200 C.E.

A mere decade or two later, Rav – a student of R. Yehuda HaNasi – left the land of Israel and settled in *Bavel*. This spawned a tremendous period of growth for the Jewish community in *Bavel*. The subsequent period of Torah scholarship, led by the *Amoraim* (200 C.E. – 500), saw *Bavel* as the major center of Jewish learning, and led to the codification of the *Talmud Bavli*. This Babylonian tradition of Torah leadership was continued by the *Geonim*, who led the *Bavel Yeshivos* in Sura and Pumbedisa, and flourished for close to half a millennium (600 – 1000).

During the time of the *Geonim* and earlier, a host of reasons drove small groups of Jews to venture from the Jewish center in *Bavel* and join the Jewish communities in the Mediterranean port cities of Europe and along the coast

---

[5] Tradition records the emergence at this time of communities in modern-day Italy, Greece, Spain, Tunisia, France, and even Germany. See Radak, *Ovadiah* 1:20. See also *Mishna Bava Basra* 38a and *Menachos* 110a in the name of Rav.

of North Africa. Responsa of the *Geonim* record a flow of letters between these outlying communities and the *Bavel yeshivos*. In these communications, the outlying communities sent *halachic* inquiries, Talmud questions, as well as other queries relating to issues of faith and *hashkafa*. While some of these communities may have been major Torah centers,[6] most were seemingly bereft of significant Torah scholars.

In the 10th century, things began to change. The outlying communities of Europe and North Africa began to develop independency from *Bavel*. Their communities grew in size, and their level of Torah scholarship increased. At the same time, the *Bavel yeshivos* were also beginning to wane in influence and prestige. These new realities ushered in the period of the *Rishonim*.

We will be discussing the transmission of the Talmudic tradition in the period of the early Rishonim, which covers the 11th and 12th centuries.

---

[6] For example, there was apparently a very rich Torah culture in Italy at this time. The *Geonim* make references to the "Yeshiva of Rome," and the *Rishonim* speak of the great Torah scholars that had once flourished in the cities of Bari and Otranto.

THE EARLY RISHONIM OF NORTH AFRICA

A 12TH CENTURY RABBINIC HISTORY BOOK called *Sefer HaKabbalah* tells the fateful tale of a ship that set sail from Bari, Italy. On the boat were several distinguished Rabbi seeking funds for charity. The boat was hijacked, and its passengers were taken captive. Four of these Torah scholars were ransomed by coastal communities on the Mediterranean. According to this tradition, the redeemed Rabbis remained in those cities and contributed greatly to their learning centers.

One of the four captives was R. Chushiel of Italy (d. 1027), who was ransomed by the Jewish community in Kairouan, North Africa. R. Chushiel was a leading *talmid chacham*, who had likely studied under the *Geonim*. After being redeemed by the Kairouan community, R. Chushiel remained there and eventually headed the Kairouan *yeshiva*.[7]

---

[7] There are historical sources that indicate that R. Chushiel arrived in Karouian on his own free will around the year 1005. To resolve this discrepancy, it has been suggested that after being ransomed R. Chushiel left Kairouan and then returned on his own free will. That

The communities in North Africa maintained a strong connection with the *Bavel yeshivos*. With Egypt serving as the gateway to the Maghreb,[8] major travel routes existed from the Babylonian region to North Africa. The constant traffic linked the new Torah centers of North Africa with the centuries-old *Bavel* center.[9]

General Historical Overview

For hundreds of years the coast of North Africa was ruled by the Carthaginian Empire. Their capital, Carthage,

---

R. Chushiel had Italian roots is supported by an extant responsum he signed along with other rabbinic figures from Bari, Italy.

[8] The "Maghreb" is the northern region of Africa, excluding the eastern most segment where Egypt is located. The Mediterranean coastline of the Maghreb was an important tract of land throughout history as it was home to many important port cities.

[9] One area where this had a major impact on Talmud study was the text of the Talmud. It is theorized that due to their connection with *Bavel*, the North African Talmudists had excellent editions of the Talmud Bavli. Whenever the text of a passage was in question, the North African Talmudists were able to send a letter to *Bavel* and in a relatively short interval of time receive clarification of the proper text. The issue of the proper text of the Talmud (*girsa*) was a major issue in the Ashkenazic Torah centers in northern Europe. Lacking a direct connection with *Bavel*, the Ashkenazim were forced to conjecture the proper text of the Talmud. But in North Africa, it seems, the contact with *Bavel* allowed the North African Talmudists to enjoy a more authoritative edition of the Talmud.

was on the outskirts of the modern-day city of Tunis.[10] But in 146 B.C.E., Carthage fell to Rome in the Punic Wars, and the Romans took control of the Maghreb coast.

For most of the period of the *Tanaaim* (100 B.C.E. – 200 C.E.) and *Amoraim* (200 – 500), the Maghreb was part of the Roman Empire. In the 5th Century, the region was conquered by the Vandals, a Germanic Tribe that had embraced Arian Christianity in the 4th century.[11] The Vandals held control of the coast of North Africa until the 6th century, when the Eastern Roman Empire led by Justinian gained control of the coast. In the 7th century, Muslim forces from Egypt invaded and conquered the coast of North Africa, and by the beginning of the 8th century, the expanding Muslim empire occupied all of Spain and their rule even extended into France. Although Christian forces slowly pushed the Muslims out of Spain, the egion remained in Muslim hands for centuries.

---

[10] Carthage was originally a city-state of a Semitic people called the Phoenicians. They were from the city of Tyre (צור) and the general region of modern-day Lebanon. In circa 650 B.C.E., the Carthaginians gained independence from the Phoenicians and established an empire on a significant part of the western coast of North Africa.

[11] Arianism was a form of Christianity based on the teachings of Arius (d. 336). His teachings were at odds with the Roman Catholic Church and were deemed heretical by mainstream Christianity.

R. Yaakov and R. Nisim of Kairouan

R. Yaakov b. Nisim (d. 1010) was *Rosh Yeshiva* in Kairouan when R. Chushiel arrived in Kairouan. In extant collections of Geonic responsa, there are several *teshuvos* sent from Rav Sherira Gaon, and his son Rav Hai Gaon, in *Bavel* to Rav Yaakov in Kairouan. The most famous *teshuva* was in response to an inquiry sent by R. Yaakov in the year 987 to the *Geonim* in *Bavel* on behalf of the Kairouan community. In the letter, Rav Yaakov requested an elaboration of the *masorah* from Moshe Rabbenu until the redaction of the *Mishna*. The response, known as the *Igeres Rav Sherira Gaon*, became a classic text in the study of the *masorah*.

R. Yaakov's son, Rabbenu Nisim Gaon (d. 1060) was another important rabbinic figure from North Africa at this time. R. Nisim studied under Rav Hai Gaon in Sura and was given the honorific title "*Gaon*," even though he was not actually one of the Babylonian *Geonim*.

R. Nisim Gaon wrote a Talmud commentary called *Sefer HaMafteach LeManulei HaTalmud*. The commentary focused on "unlocking" specific complicated passages by providing necessary background information not included in the Talmudic discussion. *Sefer HaMafteach LeManulei HaTalmud* is printed in the margins of standard editions of the Talmud on tractates *Berachos*, *Shabbos*, and *Eruvin* under the title, "Rav Nisim Gaon." The introduction to the *sefer* is printed in standard edition of the Talmud on tractate *Berachos*.

R. Nisim also wrote a halachic work called *Megilas Setarim*. This work has generally been lost, but a few fragments have been discovered. The *Megilas Setarim is* quoted a number of times by the printed *Tosafos*, where R. Nisim's interpretations of the Talmud and his halachic rulings are documented and analyzed.

R. Chananel b. Chushiel (רבינו חננאל)

When R. Yaakov passed away, R. Chushiel succeeded him as *Rosh Yeshiva* in Kairouan. This position was then passed on to R. Chushiel's son, Rabbenu Chananel (d. 1056). R. Chananel was greatly influenced by the Geonic teachings, which were dominant in Kairouan at that time, plus the Italian tradition he had learned from his father.

R. Chananel's major work was a running commentary on the Talmud. In general, R. Chananel's commentary explains and summarizes the Talmudic discussion and then concludes with a *halachic* ruling on the issue under discussion. His commentary prominently features teachings from the *Talmud Yerushalmi* and the *Geonim*.[12]

It appears that R. Chananel's commentary was only written on those *Sedarim* that were relevant to daily life: *Mo'ed*, *Nezikin*, *Nashim*, plus tractates *Berachos* and *Chullin*.[13] Unlike earlier commentaries of the *Geonim* that focused on specific difficult passages, R. Chananel's

---

[12] At times, R. Chananel even quotes directly from R. Hai Gaon without even mentioning his name.

[13] Originally his commentary was only known through quotations from others, but in the 18th century the text of his commentary was included on the page of the standard Talmud on a number of tractates.

commentary was a running commentary that covered every *sugya*. R. Chananel's commentary was also unique in that it was written in Hebrew, not Arabic like many of the commentaries of the *Geonim*.[14]

During the 11th and first half of the 12th centuries, R. Chananel's commentary was the dominant commentary in Sephardic lands, and, by the middle of the 12th century, R. Chananel's commentary had penetrated the Ashkenazic circles of northern Europe.

R. Chananel's commentary had a significant influence on later Talmudists. For example, R. Nosson b. Yechiel of Rome (d. 1106), the author of an important and highly influential Talmudic dictionary called the *Sefer HaAruch*, quotes often from R. Chananel's commentary. We will see shortly that R. Yitzchak Alfasi (Rif) was influenced by R. Chananel, as were the Talmudists of Provence and the French *Ba'alei Tosafos*.[15]

R. Yitzchak Alfasi (ר״יף)

R. Yitzchak (d. 1102), known as the Rif, lived much of his life in the city of Fez (in present day Morocco), and for this reason he is called *Al-fasi*. He was a student of R. Chananel

---

[14] R. Chananel's commentary does feature a few Arabic and Greek words, much like Rashi's commentary features French words from time to time. This is reflective of the respective influences and surroundings of the authors.

[15] The *Ba'alei Tosafos* regularly quote R. Chananel's *girsa* of the Talmudic text.

and R. Nisim Gaon.[16] For the last fifteen years of his life he lived in Spain, where he headed a *yeshiva* in the city of Lucena.[17]

The Rif's major work is called the "*Halachos Rabasi,*" known simply as the "*Halachos.*" In the *Halachos*, the Rif weaves together select statements of the Talmudic discussion. His work features a marked focus on the final conclusions of the *sugyos*, as he omitted the opinions that were rejected in the course of the Talmud's analysis and highlighted those that he thought reflected the final *pesak*. The Rif also added short statements of commentary in Aramaic.[18]

The Rif only wrote his *Halachos* on tractates that have practical *halachic* ramifications. Hence the Rif's *Halachos* was only on *Sedarim Mo'ed, Nashim,* and *Nezikin,* plus tractates *Berachos, Chullin,* and *Nidah*.[19] Even within a

---

[16] Many times when the Rif quotes from R. Chananel he writes, "איכא מאן דאמר." See for example, *Rif Succah* 2a (Rif's pagination) and the corresponding comment of R. Chananel on *Succah* 2b.

[17] The city of Lucena is in the region of Cordoba, one of the provinces of Andalusia. Other important regions in Andalusia are Seville and Granada.

[18] Occasionally, the Rif included eloquent monologues in Geonic Aramaic, and in three locations he appends long discussions in Arabic to the end of a tractate. The Rif also authored many *teshuvos*.

[19] In some instances, the Rif rearranged the placement of certain laws. For example, the laws of *Nidah* he placed in his *Halachos* on the second chapter of tractate *Shevuos*, which deals with laws of ritual impurity, and the laws of *Sefiras HaOmer* that appear in tractate *Menachos* he placed at the end of his *Halachos* on tractate *Pesachim*,

tractate, if a particular chapter did not have practical *halachic* ramifications, the Rif omitted it from his work.[20] In short, the *Halachos* is an elucidated abridgement of the Talmud and is also, in some senses, a *halachic sefer pesak*.

The Rif's rulings and appended commentary were drawn from: (1) His teachers, R. Chananel and R. Nisim, (2) The classic tradition of the later *Geonim*, such as Rav Hai Gaon, and, (3) The *Talmud Yerushalmi*. The Rif also included his own *chiddushim* into the *Halachos*.

The Rif's *Halachos* became very popular and even replaced the Talmud in many communities.[21] Many people claimed that there was no longer a point in studying all of the long-winded discussion in the Talmud. For them, study of the Rif's *Halachos* was an excellent way to learn Talmud and fulfill the dictate of Chazal: "לאסוקי שמעתתא אליבא

---

due to the seasonal relationship. The Rif also wrote "*Halachos Ketanos*" on topics in *Sedarim Kodashim* and *Taharos* that are applicable nowadays, such as the laws of writing a Torah scroll, *mezuzah, tefillin*, etc.

[20] For example, the Rif skipped chapters five through nine in tractate *Pesachim*, which deal with *korban Pesach*, and he also skipped chapters one through seven in tractate *Yuma* that deal with the *avodah* of *Yom Kippur*.

[21] **Versions of the Rif's Halachos:** The Rif wrote the *Halachos* in Fez, but after immigrating to Spain, the Rif continued to update and edit the *Halachos*. It is important to realize that due to communication and printing limitations the *Rishonim* generally publicized changes and updates through letters to students. Hence, there are many versions of the Rif, all with different degrees of inclusion of the updates and corrections.

דהילכתא."[22] It is for this reason the *Halachos* were nicknamed *Talmud Katan*.

Even for those who did not see the Rif's work as a replacement of the Talmud, the *Halachos* still occupied a central role in study. In the 12th century, the Rif was considered the main *posek* of the Sephardic communities and Provence, and the Rambam follows him consistently, claiming to argue with him on only a few points.

Many super-commentaries were authored on the Rif. In fact, many famous Talmudic commentaries were actually written on the Rif's *Halachos* and not on the Talmud. For example, the *Piskei HaRosh* and the commentaries of the Ran and Nimukei Yosef all use the Rif's *Halachos* as the springboard for their works.

It is reported that the Vilna Gaon encouraged his students to "learn the Rif every day, and review it well."[23] A student writes, "I received my approach to learning from the great *Gaon*, our teacher Eliyahu of Vilna, who commanded me with his holy mouth to learn the Rif with Rashi and to constantly review it."[24]

---

[22] **"Rashi's Commentary" on the Rif:** A testament to the popularity of the *Halachos* is the fact that Rashi's commentary was appended to printed editions of the Rif's work. Rashi did not write a commentary on the *Halachos*, but due to the overwhelming popularity of the Rif's work, printers appended relevant passages from Rashi's commentary to the page of the *Halachos* to aid in its study.

[23] *Sefer Hanhagos HaGra* and *Ma'aseh Rav* #60 (quoted in the introduction to *Sefer Shvil HaZahav*).

[24] *Sefer Rosh HaGivah* (ibid.).

The End of the Early Rishonim in N. Africa

Toward the end of the Rif's life, the Rif moved north to southern Spain. This move reflected a shift in the Torah center that was undoubtedly linked to the harsh decrees against the Jews in North Africa towards the end of the 11th century. Not until the 14th century will we find major Torah personalities returning to North Africa.[25]

In concluding, it is significant to note that, in general, the early Talmud commentaries of North Africa were paraphrases or abridgments of the Talmudic discussion. In a sense, one could read through these commentaries with minimal use, or even no use, of the Talmud itself.[26] We will soon see that in Ashkenaz a very different style was utilized, one that *accompanied* the text of the Talmud and could not be understood without the text itself.

---

[25] *Sefer HaKabbalah* states that after the Rif, Torah study left N. Africa and moved northward to Spain. Nonetheless, there were still some great Talmudists in N. Africa after the Rif. For example, R. Ephraim was a student of the Rif who wrote a spirited super-commentary on the Rif. In many cases, R. Ephraim defends R Chananel from the Rif's attacks. Some of his comments were erroneously included in the main text of the Rif's *Halachos* by later printers. Another example is R. Zechariah (d. 1195), from the city of Agmat, Morocco. R. Zechariah compiled *Sefer HaNer*, a super-commentary on the Rif. *Sefer HaNer* is the first work of the *Shitah Mekubetzes* genre, a digest of commentaries on the Talmudic discussion.

[26] R. Chananel often summarized the *sugya*, R. Nisim wrote a complete paraphrase, and the Rif abridged and edited the *sugyos*.

THE EARLY RISHONIM OF SOUTHERN SPAIN

TRADITION RELATES THAT JEWS CAME to Spain during the time of the *churban*. Certainly by the time of the *Mishna*, there was already a Jewish settlement in Spain.[27] However, until the Arab conquest of Spain in 711 C.E. we hear very little about Torah learning in Spain. At this point, we begin to find records of a relationship between the communities of Spain and the *yeshivos* in *Bavel*. In fact, tradition records that in 770, R. Natronai b. Chachinai left *Bavel* and settled in the Iberian Peninsula. In Spain, he wrote from memory a copy of the Talmud, and initiated a major increase in Talmud study.[28] As Torah study increased in Spain, the connection to the *yeshivos* in *Bavel* increased. Indeed, the ninth century witnessed increased *Teshuvos* arriving in Spain from Sura and Pumbedisa.

However, a major change in the Spanish Torah center occurred with the arrival of R. Moshe b. Chanoch (d. 965). Like R. Chushiel, R. Moshe was one of the "four captives" on

---

[27] See *Bava Basra* 38a.

[28] Reported by R. Shmuel HaNagid.

the pirated ship from Italy. The community in Cordoba, Spain ransomed R. Moshe, and he established a Torah center there that attracted many students. With the establishment of his *Beis Midrash*, Spain gained a degree of independence from *Bavel*. This independence continued with R. Moshe's son, R. Chanoch.[29]

In the following generations, Spain was home to illustrious Torah scholars. The most famous being R. Chanoch's student, R. Shmuel HaNagid (d. 1056), and his student, R. Yitzchak Ibn Gayas (d. 1089). Although these great scholars were contemporaries of R. Chananel and the Rif, remnants of their works are scarce. Save for some references in the writings of other *Rishonim*, little is left of their legacy.

General Historical Overview

Andalusia is the southern region of Spain, situated along the Mediterranean coast. During the time of the *Mishna* and *Gemara*, Andalusia was part of the Roman Empire. In the 4th century, the Roman Empire officially converted to Christianity, and hence Spain fell under the influence of the Christian Church of Rome. In the 5th and 6th century, Spain was conquered by the Visigoths, and their rule extended to Andalusia. The Visigoths were a Germanic tribe that had pagan roots, but had been

---

[29] **R. Chasdai Ibn Shaprut:** A well-known contemporary of R. Moshe was R. Chasdai Ibn Shaprut (d. late 10th century). R. Chasdai lived in Cordoba and was a very influential adviser (and physician) to the Caliph, and also acted as a minister of foreign affairs.

Christianized before arriving in Spain. Hence, under the Visigoths, Spain remained under the general influence of Christianity.[30] This changed in the year 711 when the Moors (indigenous Muslims of North Africa) penetrated the Spanish coast and established an Islamic state (Caliphate) in southern Spain. In the 10th century, Christian warriors from the north began to wrestle control from the Muslims with the goal of reconquering Spain. For the next 500 years, Spain was the battleground between the Christians in the north and the Muslims in the south, with the Jews often caught in the middle. However, during most of the period of the early *Rishonim* Andalusia was ruled by Muslim dynasties.[31]

R. Shmuel HaNagid (ר' שמואל הנגיד)

R. Shmuel HaNagid (d. 1056) was a major Talmud scholar, a poet, and perhaps the greatest political figure in the Jewish history of Muslim Spain. He was appointed vizier (political advisor/minister) to the Berber king in Granada,

---

[30] The Visigoths first converted to Arianism and then, in the late 6th century, to Catholicism. Sources indicate that the Jews were treated well when the Visigoths were Arians, but that this changed drastically when the Visigoths became Catholics.

[31] In the late 13th century most of Andalusia fell to the Christian Reconquista, but it was not until the late 15th century that the Christians succeeded in ridding Spain completely of Muslim dominion.

24 • THE EARLY RISHONIM

Andalusia, and at the same time was the leader of Spanish Jewry.[32]

R. Shmuel authored a number of important *seforim*. His Talmud commentary was not a comprehensive commentary on entire tractates, rather it focused on challenging *sugyos*. It drew heavily from the Geonic tradition, and although no longer extant, it is the first known work on the Talmud written on Spanish soil.[33] R. Shmuel's most famous work, was a *halachic* work on issues relating to daily life called *Hilchos HaNagid* or *Hilchasa Gavrevasa*. It, too, is no longer extant, but it is quoted by other *Rishonim*.

R. Yitzchak Ibn Gayas (רי"ץ גיות)

R. Yitzchak Ibn Gayas (d. 1089) succeeded his teacher, R. Shmuel HaNagid, as a rabbinic leader in Andalusian Spain. He was a *Rosh Yeshiva* in Lucena and, in this role, may have been a teacher of the Rif, who served as *Rosh Yeshiva* in Lucena after R. Yitzchak passed away.

R. Yitzchak was very prolific and left many works. He wrote a Talmud commentary in Arabic called ספר סראג',

---

[32] R. Shmuel's son, Rav Yosef, married the daughter of R. Nissim Gaon and succeeded R. Shmuel as vizier in Granada. In 1066, a Muslim mob rampaged through Granada and massacred many Jews. The mob also stormed the royal palace, and Rav Yosef was killed *al kiddush Hashem*.

[33] R. Shmuel's Talmud commentary is basically contemporaneous to the first known Talmud commentary written in Christian Europe, the *perush* of Rabbenu Gershom.

which in Hebrew is *Sefer HaNer*.³⁴ The commentary focuses primarily on hard words and concepts in the Talmud. R. Yitzchak also wrote a halachic work called *Halachos Kelulos*, but printed under the title *Sha'arei Simchah*. It is heavily based on the *Geonim*, with many verbatim quotes from Geonic works, but through the prism of the Spanish tradition, especially the teachings of his teacher, R. Shmuel.

R. Yosef ibn Migash (ר״י מיגאש)

R. Yosef, known as the Ri Migash (ר״י מיגאש), was from Seville, Spain. As a child he learned under his father and R. Yitzchak ibn Albalia of Seville, one of the great Sephardic scholars of the generation. When Ri was twelve years old, the Rif arrived in Lucena from North Africa, and the Ri left Seville to study with the Rif in Lucena. For fourteen years the Ri Migash studied with the Rif. Upon the death of the Rif in 1103, R. Yosef assumed the position of *Rosh Yeshiva* in Lucena. He led the *yeshiva* in this role for thirty-eight years until his death.

Ri Migash's greatness was described by the Rambam as follows: "That man's intellectual abilities are frightening to one who studies his words and realizes the depths of his thinking. We can apply to his style and approach in learning [the verse in Kings II 23:25], "Before him there had never been a king like him.""³⁵

---

³⁴ Not to be confused with the *Sefer HaNer* of R. Zechariah Agamati.

³⁵ Rambam, *Introduction to the Mishna*.

Ri Migash's Talmud commentary is the first *complete* commentary we have that was written on Spanish soil. His commentary was unique in Spain due to his comprehensive treatment of a tractate and his dialectic style of analysis.[36] Indeed, the Meiri describes the Ri Migash's commentary as the beginning of a new genre in Spain to include analysis with *pesak*. This was unlike many of the commentaries that were produced at this time in Spain, which focused solely on *pesak* or on explaining specific hard words, concepts, or passages. Still, Ri Migash's commentary is heavily based on his predecessors, although he does not always quote them by name. When he does, he most often references the Rif (whom he calls רבינו), R. Chananel, and R. Hai Gaon.

While there are indications that Ri Migash wrote his commentary on many tractates, only tractates *Shevuos* and

---

[36] **Dialectic Talmud Study:** In the context of Talmud study, "dialectic study" refers to a rigorous style of analysis that questioned every aspect of a Talmudic discussion. The Talmudic dialecticians would scrutinize every step of a Talmudic passage. They questioned the passage's assumptions, challenged the logic of a suggested answer, and even raised skepticism about reported teachings. Beyond the fine reading of the Talmudic text, the dialecticians would often question a Talmudic passage based on information learned from a Talmudic discussion in another location. The position of the Talmud in one tractate would be used to question the validity of a passage in another tractate, leaving the dialectician to uncover a creative resolution. Later dialecticians would put the same rigor into their analysis of the work of the earlier dialecticians.

Bava Basra are extant. In fact, the *Rishonim* also seem to only have had his commentary on these two tractates.[37]

Ri Migash maintained a correspondence with the Rabbis of Narbonne, Provence. He is the first known direct connection between the Torah leaders of Spain and those of Provence.

R. Moshe b. Maimon (רמב״ם)

R. Moshe, the Rambam (d. 1204), studied under his father, R. Maimon. R. Maimon was a student of Ri Migash, and he passed on to his son many of the Ri Migash's teachings. Legend records one meeting between the Ri Migash and a very young Rambam, who was only around six years old at the former's death.

The Rambam's early years were spent in Cordova, Spain. However, the northward expansion of the Muslims tribes

---

[37] Meiri writes that he is only in possession of Ri Migash's commentary on *Shevuos* and *Bava Basra*. It has been suggested that only Ri Migash's commentaries on these two tractates were written in Hebrew, and hence were treasured by Talmudists in all regions. The rest were written in the local Arabic, and therefore did not survive. The commentary on *Bava Basra* only survived in fragments. The current edition (edited by R. Moshe Shmuel Shapiro zt"l) is a mixture of the original fragments augmented with passages from *Shitah Mekubetzes* and *Sefer HaNer* of Rav Zechariah Agamati. The *Rishonim* also reference a work by the Ri Migash called *Megilas Setarim*. The nature of this work is not clear. It may have been on complicated *sugyos*, but others suggest that it was critical comments on the Rif's *Halachos*.

that overran North Africa in the 11th and 12th centuries created waves of persecution in southern Spain during the Rambam's childhood and adolescence. For many of those years the Rambam's family wandered across southern Spain, eventually crossing into North Africa to hide from the Muslim persecution. After a short stay in *Eretz Yisrael*, the Rambam settled in Fustat, Egypt. For over 35 years the Rambam stood at the center of Torah Judaism in Egypt. His talents were also noticed by the gentile community, and he was appointed to be the Caliph's personal physician.

The Rambam relates that he authored a Talmud commentary on almost all of *Sedarim Mo'ed, Nashim*, and *Nezikin*, and on tractate *Chullin*. His commentary was written before he arrived in Egypt and was seemingly based on the teachings and Torah tradition that his father received from the Ri Migash. However, all we have is fragments from the Rambam's students who learned with him in his home. In a letter to the Rabbis of Lunel, the Rambam writes that he did not want to publicize his commentary because he did not have time to edit it to the degree he would have liked.

Perush HaMishna

One of the Rambam's great works is his *Commentary on the Mishna* (*Perush HaMishna*). The bulk of it was written in his early years in Spain and N. Africa. The final touches were done when he arrived in Egypt in 1168, but, even then, he continued to update it with changes and alterations. In fact, the Rambam wrote years later of his need to make corrections due to mistakes, which he attributes to the influence of certain early commentaries that he studied.

The Rambam's *Perush HaMishna* focuses on *pesak* and explanations and is not dialectic or analytical in nature. The work reflects a vision the Rambam had of independent *Mishna* study for the masses, something he outlines in his *Introduction to the Mishna*. The Rambam's choice to write his commentary in Arabic also seemingly reflects its intended popular audience.[38] The commentary is the first attempt to create a tool for studying *Mishna* alone, but through the prism of the Talmudic tradition. The Rambam also states that the *Perush* is an excellent tool for review.[39]

---

[38] **The Hebrew Translation of the Rambam's *Perush HaMishna*:** Toward the end of the Rambam's life, R. Yehuda Alcharizi translated select parts of the *Perush* at the request of the Rabbis of Marseille, Provence. Additionally, R. Yehuda ibn Tibbon translated the *Perush* on tractate *Avos* during the Rambam's life. But the rest of the *Perush* was not translated until the 1300's, when the Rabbis of Italy sent an emissary to the Rashba in Catalonia to help find a translator. Eventually he succeeded and a translation was fashioned through the work of various individuals. The *Perush* that is printed in the standard Talmud is an amalgamation of the various translations. The fact that it is a translation and not the Rambam's own words, plus the fact that different parts were translated by different people who did not necessarily consult one another, should be kept in mind when drawing a conclusion or making an inference from the *Perush*.

[39] Another important 12th century Mishna commentary was authored by **R Yitzchak b. Malki-Zedek of Simponto** (d. c1150), also know as the Ribmatz (ריבמ"ץ). R. Yitzchak's commentary is on the *Sedarim Zeraim* and *Taharos*. It was one of the first known commentaries on the Mishna in Europe. The prolific Tosafist R. Shimshon of Shantz, the author of a Mishna commentaries on these two *Sedarim*, was seemingly very influenced by R. Yitzchak's work. R. Yitzchak's

Included in the Rambam's *Perush HaMishna* are a number of "Introductions" that he appended to the text and have become classic works unto themselves.

1. The *Introduction to the Mishna*, or more correctly titled the *Introduction to Seder Zeraim*, discusses the nature of the Sinaitic revelation and the *Masorah*, the nature of prophecy, and it digresses to speak of the purpose of mankind.
2. The *Introduction to Tractate Avos*, known as *Shemonah Perakim*, discusses the Rambam's philosophy of man and the nature of man's soul.
3. The *Introduction to Perek Chelek*, the last chapter of tractate *Sanhedrin*, is where the Rambam discusses the nature of the "World to Come (עולם הבא)" and presents his famous Thirteen Principles of Faith.
4. The *Introduction to Seder Taharos* is a detailed overview of the laws of ritual purity.

The Mishna Torah

The Rambam's *magnum opus* in *halachah* was his fourteen-volume work, known as the *Mishna Torah*, or the *Yad HaChazakah* (the word *"yad"* is spelled *"yud-dalet,"* which is the number fourteen). Completed in his early forties and written in Hebrew, the *Mishna Torah* records the rulings of the entire Talmudic corpus and organizes them into topical sections. It is a work of colossal significance, as the Talmud itself is not organized topically. The discussions in the Talmud contain innumerable digressions, and it is nearly

---

commentary is printed in standard editions of the Talmud on *Seder Zeraim*.

impossible for a novice to emerge from a page of Talmud with a comprehensive understanding of a given topic. Seemingly, to remedy this, the Rambam wrote the *Mishna Torah*. As he writes in his introduction, a student can theoretically study the Torah and then skip right to the *Mishna Torah* for clarity of any Torah topic.[40]

The *Mishna Torah* is primarily a code and does not include the Rambam's sources for his rulings. Yet, one can extrapolate – through careful study – how the Rambam understood the relevant Talmudic discussion. For this reason, it is very popular to study the Rambam and attempt to infer the Rambam's interpretation of the Talmudic discussion. But for this very reason, the *Mishna Torah* also met much initial criticism. His detractors criticized his lack of sources, to say the least. In fact, the Rambam wrote in a letter that he was working on a source book for the *Mishna Torah*. Even if he wrote it, it is not extant. Therefore, it was left to the Rambam's commentators, such as the *Magid Mishna* and the *Kesef Mishna*, to remedy this problem by reconstructing how the Rambam arrived at his rulings.

Other Works

The Rambam also wrote *Sefer HaMitzvos*, which is his list of the biblical commandments. It begins with a presentation

---

[40] It is no surprise that the Rambam was accused of trying to supplant the Talmud. The Rambam himself writes in his introduction to *Mishna Torah* that person can read the written Torah and then directly turn to his *Mishna Torah* (skipping the *Gemara*!) and have access to the full gamut of *Torah SheBa'al Peh*.

on how to properly determine which commandments to count in the formal list of 613 commandments. As the Rambam himself writes in his introduction, the work is a critique of the *Halachos Gedolos*, a list compiled by the Geonic sage R. Shimon Kayyara. Like the *Perush HaMishna*, the *Sefer HaMitzvos* was written in Arabic in the Rambam's younger years.

Additional works of the Rambam include his major work in philosophy, the *Moreh Nevuchim*, written in Arabic and after the *Mishna Torah*, several responsa and letters, and some important medical treatises.

The End of the Early Rishonim in Spain

Torah in southern Spain went on a hiatus with the death of the Ri Migash and the departure of the Rambam. The arrival of the aforementioned Muslim tribes from North Africa drove most of the Jewish community into exile. While some were murdered, such as the author of *Sefer HaKabbalah*, R. Avraham ibn Daud (Raavad I), most fled north toward Christian lands – settling in central and northern Spain or Catalonia. In fact, the children of Ri Migash relocated the great *yeshiva* of Lucena – previously led by the Ritz Gayas, Rif, and Ri Migash – to Toledo in Central Spain. In the coming generations, some of the greatest luminaries of the Torah world were the heads of the Toledo community.[41]

---

[41] In fact, the departure of the Rambam is the end of the history of the *Rishonim* in Muslim Spain. For the rest of the period, the Spanish *Rishonim*, operated only in Christian Spain.

Early Rishonim of N. Africa and Spain

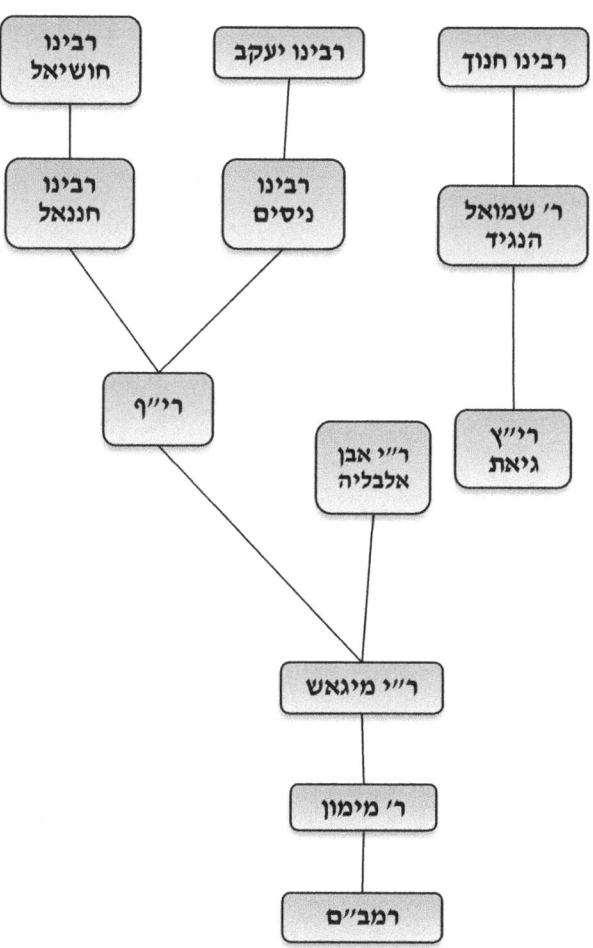

THE EARLY RISHONIM OF ASHKENAZ

JEWS LIVED IN GERMANY FOR hundreds of years before the period of the *Rishonim*. However, it is unclear when Germany started to become a Torah center. It is known that in the middle of the 9th century, members of the illustrious Kalonymus family left Italy and settled in the Rhineland. This undoubtedly contributed to the growth of Torah in the region. However, other sources indicate that some of the most influential Talmudists in the Rhineland came directly from the Babylonian *yeshivos*. Certainly, by the year 1000 a major Torah center existed in Germany.[42]

The Torah center of Germany consisted of three primary cities in the heart of the Rhineland: (1) Worms, ורמיזא or גרמיזא, (2) Mainz, מיינץ or מגנצא, and (3) Speyer, שפירא.[43]

---

[42] The early history of the Torah community in Germany is recorded by R. Shlomo Luria (Maharshal) in his *Teshuvos Maharshal* # 29.

[43] The *Sefer Or Zaruah* (*Teshuvos* 1:752) writes, "The Rabbis of Mainz, Worms, and Speyer were great scholars and holy individuals, and from [those cities] Torah went out to all of Israel…"

These cities were known by their Hebrew acronym as the "Communities of Shum (קהילות שו״מ)."

General Historical Overview[44]

During the period of the *Tanaaim*, the Roman Empire ruled over what is present day France (then known as Gaul), but was unable to subdue the various Germanic tribes that ruled in present day Germany. Toward the end of the period of the *Amoraim*, a confederation of tribes based in the Rhineland united into the Frankish Kingdom. During the following centuries, the Christianized Franks were successful in conquering territory that covered much of present-day France and Germany. At the height of their conquests under the leadership of Charlemagne (d. 814) the Franks extended the borders of their empire and ruled over much of western Europe, including the territories of present-day France, Germany, Switzerland, Belgium, the Netherlands, northern Italy, and significant parts of Austria and the Czech Republic. Upon Charlemagne's death, his empire split into smaller empires.

Throughout the period of the *Rishonim*, Ashkenazic Jewry lived in the remnants of Charlemagne's empire. The

---

[44] In the context of our discussion, the term "Ashkenaz" refers to the region of present day Germany and France. As noted above, the main Jewish Torah center in the period before the *Rishonim* was based in the Rhineland of Germany. The "Rhineland" refers to the western region of modern day Germany that is situated along the Rhine River. In the period of the *Rishonim*, Torah centers began to emerge in what is now France and the eastern region of Germany.

eastern region became the Kingdom of Germany and formed the bulk of the newly formed "Holy Roman Empire." The Jews there suffered greatly during the time of the *Rishonim*, as they were frequent victims to merciless crusaders and Christian marauders.

The western region of Charlemagne's Empire eventually formed into the Kingdom of France, and throughout the period of the *Rishonim*, France was ruled by the Kings of France. Although the Jews in France fared better than their brethren in Germany, the Jews were expelled in 1182 only to be recalled in 1198, expelled again in 1306 and recalled again in 1315, and then expelled for good in 1394.

Rabbenu Gershom (רבינו גרשום)[45]

R. Gershom (d. 1040) was called by the later *Rishonim*, "The Light of the Exile" (מאור הגולה).[46] He founded *Yeshivas Megence* (ישבית מגנצא), the first known *yeshiva* in northern Europe. In Mainz, R. Gershom served not only as *Rosh Yeshiva*, but also as a communal leader. He is well known for his communal enactments, which he strengthened via a

---

[45] *Teshuvos Maharshal* #29 lists this year as the death date of R. Gershom, making Rashi's birth and R. Gershom's death the same year, a fulfillment of the verse "The sun rises and the sun sets." (*Koheles* 1:5) However, there are other sources that list 1028 as his death date.

[46] R. Gershom studied under R. Yehuda HaKohen Leontin, who likely arrived in the Rhineland from Italy or southern France.

cherem. R. Gershom was very prolific and authored works in many areas of Torah.

In the printed editions of the *Gemara*, a commentary ascribed to R. Gershom appears in the margins of a number of tractates, including *Ta'anis*, *Bava Basra*, *Chullin*, *Erchin*, *Temurah*, and *Krisus*. However, this commentary was not written by R. Gershom himself, but is rather a product of his *yeshiva* and his students and would be more appropriately titled, "*Perush Megence*."[47] These commentaries of the Megence *yeshiva* were written in the second half of the 11th century and beginning of the 12th century.

The German Yeshivos

After the establishment of the *yeshiva* in Mainz, *yeshivos* were opened in Worms and Speyer, as Torah scholars and scholarship flourished along the Rhine River. The Torah scholars in Ashkenaz were known for their deep piety, and were referred to as *chasidim* (חסידים).[48] The early Talmud commentaries that emerged from the German *yeshivos* were paraphrases of the Talmud with additional notes and

---

[47] For example, it has been argued that the "*Perush R. Gershom*" that appears in *Bava Basra* was actually written by R. Elyakim b. Meshullum, a student of R. Gershom.

[48] This was a general term for the early scholars of Germany. Hence, we find that the Rabbis in early Ashkenaz are called "*HaChasid*," like R. Yitzchak HaChasid or R. Yehoshua HaChasid. Similarly, we find references to the "*Chasidei Mainz*" (*Sefer Aruch*, ערך אב י'). In the 12th century, a specific movement emerged called the "Chasidei Ashkenaz." They will be discussed shortly.

insights, similar in this sense to the early works from North Africa. The *yeshivos* and communities of early Ashkenaz were all led by students of R. Gershom.[49]

R. Shlomo b. Yitzchak (רש"י)

R. Shlomo Yitzchaki (d.1105), Rashi, was born in France but at a young age travelled to Germany to learn in the *yeshivos* headed by the students of R. Gershom.[50] After his *yeshiva* studies in Germany, Rashi returned to France and opened a *yeshiva* in Troyes, a town situated in the Champagne region, approximately 100 miles southeast of Paris. There Rashi led the community as *Rosh Yeshiva* and *posek*.[51]

An entire Torah community sprouted from Rashi's return to France. Rashi had three daughters, who all married great scholars. His sons-in-law, grandsons, and students were

---

[49] This included R. Elyakim b. Meshulum ("The *Moreh*"), R. Eliezer HaGadol, R. Ya'akov ben Yakar, R. Yitzchak HaLevi, and R. Yitzchak b. Yehuda.

[50] Rashi first studied in Mainz under R. Ya'akov b. Yakar (d. 1064), whom he called "*Mori HaZaken*." After R. Ya'akov's death, Rashi studied under R. Yitzchak b. Yehuda, whom he he called "*Mori Zedek*." Rashi then went to Worms and studied under R. Yitzchak haLevi, known as "סגן לויה."

[51] There are literally hundreds of rulings recorded in Rashi's *teshuvos* and those of his students. This literature is known as the ספרי דבי רש"י.

among the most illustrious rabbinic scholars and leaders of the Ashkenazi Torah community in the following century.[52]

Rashi wrote a monumental Talmud commentary that made the Talmud fully accessible for the first time. In his Talmud commentary, Rashi explained many difficult words, provided necessary background information, and, most importantly, he filled in the missing steps from a discussion that were needed to fully understand the flow of the discussion but were often absent from the actual text.

Unlike earlier works that paraphrased the Talmudic discussion, Rashi's commentary utilized the "*dibbur hamaschil*" (דיבור המתחיל) format. It focused on specific words and points, but it could not be read independently of the text. This format ensured that the Talmud student would always need the actual text of the *Gemara*. With the earlier

---

[52] Rashi's daughter Yocheved married **R. Meir**. Like his father-in-law, R. Meir also established a *yeshiva* in France. He is quoted occasionally in the printed *Tosafos* and his writings are the first to be referred to with the title "*Tosafos*" (see *Sefer HaYashar* 252). The children of R. Meir and Yocheved included Rashbam, Rabbenu Tam, and R. Yitzchak (Rivam). Rashi's daughter Miriam married **R. Yehuda ben Nosson (Rivan)**. He wrote a commentary on the Talmud, and is the author of the printed "Rashi" on tractate *Makkos* from 19b to the end of the tractate. He might also be the author of the printed "Rashi" on tractate *Nazir* and on the 10th chapter of tractate *Sanhedrin* (*Chelek*). He is also quoted in the printed *Tosafos* on at least 10 tractates.

One of Rashi's most illustrious students was **R. Simcha of Vitry** (d. 1105). He is the author of the *Machzor Vitry*, a collection of *pesakim* and *teshuvos* from Rashi and other great Ashkenazi scholars. R. Simcha's grandson was the Ri HaZaken of Dampierre, one of the greatest Tosafists.

paraphrasing format, it was possible for a Talmud student to follow the Talmudic discussion without consulting the actual text of the Talmud. However, with Rashi's format the student was unable to forgo the text. He had to study the actual Talmud *with* the commentary of Rashi. This approach likely contributed to the commentary's popularity, even with the most advanced students.[53]

It is important to realize that Rashi's commentary did not emerge from a vacuum, and the teachings within do not reflect Rashi's creativity alone. Rather, it is largely based on the teachings Rashi learned in Germany, and it reflects the rich Talmud tradition of Ashkenaz.[54]

Rashi's commentary on the Talmud revolutionized Torah learning and rapidly spread to all corners of the Torah world. It quickly became the dominant commentary in the Torah world, eclipsing all earlier works, even in Sephardic lands, where commentaries like that of R. Chananel were popular.[55]

---

[53] Because Rashi's commentary was a learning aid, people often added to it in accordance with what would help them read the Talmudic text. This led to many variant versions of Rashi's commentary. In addition, it is reported that Rashi wrote and rewrote his commentary many times. This also led to variant texts. (The first reason for variant texts mentioned here, which reflects transmission errors, is generally called "lower criticism." The second, which is due to actual authorship changes, is called "higher criticism.")

[54] Similarly, one should realize that the content of Rashi's Torah commentary is largely based on Chazal and often not Rashi's own original interpretations.

[55] **Rashi Script** – "Rashi Script" was not Rashi's creation or even from his time period. It was a later idea of the early printers in the 15th

Today, Rashi's commentary appears on the inner column of the printed *Gemara*. Although Rashi wrote on the entire Talmud, in some tractates the commentary that appears in printed editions of the Talmud is not actually Rashi's commentary:

1. *Mo'ed Katan* – The text is one of the "*Perushei Megence.*"
2. *Ta'anis* – The text is not from Rashi. It has been suggested that it is from the commentary of R. Shmuel b. Meir (Rashbam), Rashi's grandson.
3. *Nedarim* – The text is one of the "*Perushei Megence.*"
4. *Nazir* – The text is either from "*Perushei Megence*" or from the commentary of R. Yehuda b. Nosson (Rivan), Rashi's son-in-law.
5. *Bava Basra* – The text from 29a and on is from the commentary of Rashbam.
6. *Sanhedrin* – The text of the 10th chapter (*Perek Chelek*) is from the commentary of Rivan.
7. *Makkos* – The text from 19b and on is from the commentary of Rivan.

The Crusades

The Crusades were a series of Church-inspired military campaigns by European Christians to retake control of Jerusalem from its Muslim occupiers. However, on their way to the land of Israel, the merciless Crusaders destroyed scores

---

century. The purpose of the script was to differentiate between the text of the Talmud and that of Rashi.

of Jewish communities, and tortured, raped, and killed countless Jews.

Towards the end of Rashi's life, the "First Crusade" (1096-1099) ravaged the Rhineland and decimated the major Ashkenazic communities of Germany. France at this time, however, was spared destruction and continued to grow under the leadership of Rashi's *yeshiva* and family.[56] In Germany, Torah survived, but largely because young students came to France to learn in Rashi's academy.[57]

The Ba'alei Tosafos (בעלי תוספות)

After Rashi, Torah in Ashkenaz was dominated by the *Ba'alei Tosafos*. Rashi's line-by-line commentary opened the previously abstruse folios of the Talmud in an unparalleled way. However, Rashi's commentary was a local commentary that focused on the immediate discussion. He chose explanations that presented the local passage with the most

---

[56] French Jewry did not fare as well during future Crusades.

[57] One example of this phenomenon is **R. Yitzchak b. Asher HaLevi** (Riva, d. 1133). Riva was the son-in-law of R. Elyakim b. Meshulam and he served as the *Rosh Yeshiva* in Speyer. Riva studied at some point with Rashi (See *Tosafos Nidah* 15b). He wrote a *Tosafos*-style commentary on many tractates, and he was the first German whose works were referred to as "*Tosafos*." Many *Rishonim* even refer to him as "בעל התוספות" – "The Tosafist." He is quoted often in the printed *Tosafos* by his acronym ריב״א. Note: There were two people named R. Yitzchak b. Asher, one the grandson of the other. We are discussing the older R. Yitzchak.

clarity, even if this required ignoring a relevant discussion in another tractate. This was not the case with the *Ba'alei Tosafos*. Working with an assumption that the entire Talmudic corpus was one unified text – an assumption that Rashi likely agreed to but did not focus on when composing his commentary – the early *Ba'alei Tosafos* focused their work on more global, Talmud-wide analysis.[58]

With a more Talmud-wide perspective, the *Ba'alei Tosafos* studied the Talmud seeking to identify difficulties in Talmudic passages (or Rashi's explanation of Talmudic passages) based on parallel, or at least relevant, discussions in other locations. The *Ba'alei Tosafos* then suggested creative resolutions to the problems they found. The overarching goal was to unify the entire Talmud.[59]

How did the Tosafists approach each *sugya* from the perspective of the entire Talmud? In addition to reading the local discussion, they also considered every passage in light of the entire Talmudic corpus. If a relevant passage elsewhere could shed light on the current passage, or if it posed a difficulty, it was analyzed and applied to the passage at hand. More specifically, Tosafist methods consisted of cross-

---

[58] The early Tosafists were likely seeking to complement, and not replace, the commentary of their ancestor Rashi, and it could be that for this intention they received the name "*Tosafos*," meaning "additions."

[59] R. Shlomo Luria (Maharshal, d. 1574) described the Tosafists' approach as one that transformed the Talmud into a "ball" – uniting it from all sides.

referencing, resolving contradictions, and suggesting innovative readings of Talmudic passages. Hair splitting distinctions and ingenious use of *okimta* – the reduction of a principle, or limiting of a ruling, to specific parameters – were the methods that the Tosafist relied upon in their disputes over resolving and explaining contradictory Talmud passages.

However, the analysis of the Tosafist did not always draw on material from other Talmudic discussions. The Tosafists also utilized standard critical analysis in their commentary, and suggested alternate interpretations based on a careful reading of the local discussion. They also produced new works of *pesak Halacha*, based on their analysis of the Talmud.

The majority of the Tosafist flourished in northern France and Germany; however, there were also Tosafists in England and Italy. The period of the Tosafists extended over a number of generations and spanned closed to one hundred and fifty years.

The Tosafists texts that we have today are not monolithic. They differ in style, authorship, and place of origin. R. Chaim Yosef Dovid Azulai (Chida, d. 1806) writes that every Tosafist, and there were scores of them, wrote a Talmud commentary. For this reason, we hear of different *Tosafos* collections, such as the *Tosafos Shantz*, *Tosafos R. Peretz*, or *Tosafos HaRosh*. Each one is different and reflects a unique Torah tradition.

For example, the *Tosafos Shantz* were authored by the French Tosafist R. Shimshon of the city Sens (Shantz). His *Tosafos* are basically a record of the lecture of R. Yitzchak

HaZaken (Ri) with some of his own additions. However, the *Tosafos Tukh* were produced at least two generations later by R. Eliezer of Tukh in Germany. They too are based on the teachings of Ri, but also include important contributions from Ri's French students, and from mid-thirteenth century German Talmudists.

What is most significant to note is that all printed *Tosafos* commentaries contain multiple layers of teachings that reflect different authors. For example, a single *Tosafos* passage found on the page of the *Gemara* can contain a question posed by a first generation French Tosafist, an answer suggested by a third generation English Tosafist, and a problem raised with the suggested answer that was noted by a fifth generation German Tosafist.

It is also important to realize that the printed *Tosafos* commentaries that appear in the outer column of today's Talmud were not chosen systematically. Although, one of the earliest printers, Gershon Soncino, sought out a specific collection of *Tosafos* – the *Tosafos Tukh* – he was not entirely successful. While there are many tractates that do contain the *Tosafos Tukh* as the printed *Tosafos*, there are many other tractates that contain other *Tosafos* commentaries – such as the *Tosafos R. Peretz*, edited by R. Peretz of Corbeil, or the *Tosafos Evreux*, edited in the *yeshiva* of Evreux, France – as the printed *Tosafos*.[60]

---

[60] It is important to note that *Tosafos Tukh* is a later Tosafist work and it is based on earlier Tosafist works. Moreover, R. Eliezer of Tukh did not always use the same sources for the various tractates. For example, in some tractates *Tosafot Tukh* were based on *Tosafos Shantz*, while in other tractates *Tosafos Tukh* were based on *Tosafos R. Baruch*.

R. Shmuel b. Meir (רשב״ם)

R. Shmuel b. Meir (d. 1158) of Troyes was Rashi's grandson, and he even saw Rashi in his youth. He is well known for his commentary on the Torah that focused on the straightforward explanation of the verses, but he was also an accomplished Talmudist.

He wrote a commentary on Talmud that was influenced by his grandfather Rashi, the commentary of R. Chananel, and the commentary of the Arukh. His commentary is more long-winded than that of his grandfather Rashi. For example, Rashbam takes time to present and analyze alternate explanations, he addresses the views of the early German *yeshivos* and the *Geonim*, and he deals with many of the variant texts (*girsaos*) of the *Gemara*.

His commentary on *Bava Basra* and the tenth chapter of *Pesachim* appears in printed editions of the Talmud. His name appears in *Tosafos* throughout the Talmud, where he is referred to as "Rabbenu Shmuel."

R. Yaakov b. Meir (רבינו תם)

Rabbenu Tam (d. 1171) was Rashbam's younger brother, but never had the merit to meet his grandfather Rashi. He studied with his father, R. Meir, and his older brother,

Rashbam. Rabbenu Tam was born in Ramerupt, a city on the Seine River, and died in Rashi's city of Troyes.[61]

Rabbenu Tam was known all over the Jewish world as a scholar and influential communal leader.[62] He instituted a number of *gezeiros* when he presided over synods of the French Rabbinical leaders.

The teachings of Rabbenu Tam serve as the foundation of our *Tosafos*. In fact, many of the anonymous passages that appear in our printed *Tosafos* are his teachings. He also was a major *posek*, and he dealt with many of the pressing issues of his day, such as the increase in commercial interaction with gentiles and the tragic situations that arose regarding martyrdom and persecution.

The only remaining work we have from Rabbenu Tam is *Sefer HaYashar*.[63] The work has two sections: (1) *Teshuvos* and (2) *Chiddushim*. *Sefer HaYashar* is very useful for finding Rabbenu Tam's original verbal formulation;

---

[61] Rabbenu Tam might have left Ramerupt in response to a near death experience. On the second day of *Shevuos* (1147) Rabbenu Tam was dragged out of his house by Crusaders, and beat in a field. On the verge of death, Rabbenu Tam was saved by a passing noble who responded to Rabbenu Tam's pleas. For the account, see *Sefer Gezerios Ashkenaz VeTzarfas*, 121.

[62] In the introduction to *Yam Shel Shlomo*, it is quoted in the name of Rosh that of all the *Rishonim*, no one, not even the Rambam, was a greater scholar than Rabbenu Tam, or his nephew, the Ri.

[63] Rabbenu Tam also authored a commentary on *Iyov* and another work on Hebrew grammar. It should be noted that there is a *mussar* work ascribed to Rabbenu Tam, also called *Sefer HaYashar*, but he is apparently not the true author of that work.

however, the extant versions of the text are in poor condition and contain many scribal errors.

R. Tam's Contemporaries and Students

The Maharshal writes that Rabbenu Tam had eighty students that were all accomplished scholars ("ראוי להוראה").[64] Some of Rabbenu Tam's colleagues and students were:

R. Chaim Kohen (ר' חיים כהן)

R. Chaim Kohen lived in Paris and was a *talmid muvhak* of Rabbenu Tam. He appears in the printed *Tosafos* in at least eighteen tractates.[65] His grandson was R. Moshe of Coucy (Semag).

R. Eliezer of Metz (ר' אליעזר ממץ/רא"ם)

R. Eliezer of Metz was a *talmid muvhak* of Rabbenu Tam. He is quoted in the printed *Tosafos* in a few locations.

R. Eliezer was the author of *Sefer Yeraim*, which is primarily a halachic work structured around the 613 commandments. The work also contains "*mussar*" elements, and R. Eliezer writes of the decline in affairs of their culture

---

[64] *Yam Shel Shlomo*, introduction to tractate *Chullin*

[65] Note that sometimes ר"ח in *Tosafos* is R Chaim and not R. Chananel, see for instance *Gittin* 42b *s.v. VeShor* and compare it to *Mordechai, Bava Kamma* 8:86.

and of a lack of Torah knowledge. In structuring the work, R. Eliezer split the commandments into seven "pillars" – each pillar focusing on a different sphere of man's desires. Besides the "*mussar*" elements of the work, the *Sefer Yeraim* is still not a traditional *halachic* code or list of the commandments. R. Eliezer included many long winded dialectic *Tosafos*-style discussions in presenting each mitzvah. The *Sefer Yeraim* was instantly popular and spread very quickly across the world of Torah study.

Metz, today part of France, is relatively close to the Rhineland centers of Torah study; R. Eliezer even lived for a period of time in the city of Mainz, Germany. Hence, R. Eliezer served as an important channel for the dissemination of R. Tam's teachings in Germany. Indeed, many of the leading Talmudists of Germany in the next generation were students of R. Eliezer, including: the Ravyah, R. Simcha of Speyer, and R. Eleazar of Worms (Rokeach).

R. Shimshon HaZaken (ר' שמשון הזקן)

R. Shimshon HaZaken of Falaise was Rabbenu Tam's brother-in-law. He is quoted in the printed *Tosafos* in a number of tractates and in German halachic codes, like those of the Ravyah and Or Zaruah. He was killed *al kiddush Hashem* and was not buried for half a year (See *Sefer HaYashar, Teshuvos* 92). His grandsons were R. Shimshon of Shantz and the Ritzva.

R. Eliyahu of Paris (רבינו אליהו)

R. Eliyahu of Paris was a colleague of Rabbenu Tam. He is quoted in the printed *Tosafos* in at least fifteen tractates, and appears in many other early works of the *Rishonim*.[66]

R. Yitzchak b. Shmuel (ר״י הזקן)

Ri HaZaken (d. 1190) of Dampierre was a prolific Tosafist, perhaps more influential than even Rabbenu Tam. Ri's mother was Rabbenu Tam's sister, making him a nephew of Rabbenu Tam and a great-grandson of Rashi. On his father's side, he was a grandson of Rashi's student, R. Simcha

---

[66] Other contemporaries and students of Rabbenu Tam were: (1) **R. Yitzchak ben Meir**, a younger brother of Rashbam and Rabbenu Tam. Although he died at a young age, he appears in a number of tractates and is called at time Rivam (not to be confused with Rivam of Germany, who appears more frequently in *Tosafos*). (2) **Rabbenu Meshulam of Melun** was originally from Narbonne, Provence, however, he moved north to the Parisian suburb of Melun and engaged in heated debates with the Rabbinic establishment, especially Rabbenu Tam. R. Meshulum is quoted in the printed *Tosafos* in at least nine tractates. (3) **R. Yosef of Orleans** was known as the *Bechor Shor* after his commentary on the Torah with that title. He appears in the printed *Tosafos* as ר׳ יוסף, ר׳ יוסף מאורלייניס, or ר׳ יוסף בכור שור. ר׳ יוסף בכור שור. His granddaughter married R. Yehuda of Paris. (4) **R. Ya'akov of Orleans** was a student of Rabbenu Tam and known as "Rabbenu Tam of Orleans." He appears occasionally in the printed *Tosafos*. He was killed *al kiddush Hashem* in London by rioters during the coronation of Richard the Lionheart. (5) **R. Yosef b. Moshe Porat** was a *talmid-chaver* of Rabbenu Tam from Troyes who learned under Rashbam. He appears in *Tosafos Berachos*, *Shabbos*, and *Tosafos Yeshanim* to *Yuma*, sometimes as R. Yosef, sometimes as R. Porat.

of Vitry. Even Ri's wife was a great great-granddaughter of Rashi. Ri studied under his uncle Rashbam and R. Eliyahu of Paris. However, his primary teacher was his uncle Rabbenu Tam. In certain respects, Ri was the most central figure in the Tosafist movement. According to the Maharshal, it was the *Beis Midrash* of Ri in Dampierre, France that produced the basic framework for the French Tosafist teachings.[67] Reflecting this is the fact that Ri is quoted by name in the printed *Tosafos* commentary more than any other Tosafist.[68]

Tradition records that Ri's *Beis Midrash* featured sixty accomplished Talmud scholars – each a master of a different tractate. These scholars would sit in a circle around Ri during his *shiurim*. As Ri would discuss a *sugya* any scholar who had a relevant comment from his mastered tractate would comment and enrich the analysis of the passage at hand.[69] Ri's students copiously recorded his *shiurim* and also added their own insights. Their works are the backbone of the printed *Tosafos*.

---

[67] *Yam Shel Shlomo*, introduction to tractate *Chullin*.

[68] Another source for the Torah of Ri is the *Hagahos Ashrei* of R. Yisrael of Kremz. R. Yisrael often quotes the rulings of Ri as they are found in the *Pesakim of R. Hezkiah of Magdeburg*. R. Yisrael notes this source when he writes: פר״י מהרי״ח (= פירוש ר״י מהפסקים של ר׳ חזקיה).

It should be noted that in tractate *Kiddushin* the margin of the printed Talmud contains "*Tosafos Ri HaZaken*," yet this commentary was not written by Ri, but rather by R. Avraham Min HaHar, a 13th century Talmud scholar from Provence.

[69] *Tzedah LaDerech*, Introduction, 6.

Talmidei HaRi

Ri's students spread his teachings to all corners of Ashkenaz, and beyond. He had five primary students, each a major channel for the dissemination of the Tosafist teachings.

Rabbenu Elchanon (רבינו אלחנן)

R. Elchanon (d. 1184) was Ri's son. His greatness is often compared with that of his father. R. Elchanon was killed *al kiddush Hashem* in 1184, while his father was still alive.

R. Elchanon wrote a *Tosafos* commentary on the Talmud, and he is quoted many times in the printed *Tosafos*. There are even portions of the printed *Tosafos* that were based upon his *Tosafos* commentary, such as the *Tosafos* on the last chapter of tractate *Pesachim*. His *Tosafos* on tractate *Avodah Zarah* are extant and have been published as an independent volume.

Rabbenu Baruch (רבינו ברוך)

R. Baruch (d. 1211) lived in Germany but studied in France under Ri and R. Eliezer of Metz. Even after Ri's death, R. Baruch remained in France, and eventual immigrated to Israel in 1208.

R. Baruch wrote a *Tosafos* commentary known as *Tosafos Rabbenu Baruch*, and he is quoted occasionally in the printed

Tosafos.[70] R. Baruch is also the author of *Sefer HaTerumah*, an important halachic work that reflects many of the rulings and teachings of the early *Ba'alei Tosafos*, especially Ri. *Sefer HaTerumah* focuses on topics relating to practical *halacha*, such as *shechitah, gittin, teffilin*, etc. The *Sefer HaTerumah* was very popular and spread quickly in France, Germany, Italy, and even Spain.

R. Yitzchak b. Avraham (ריצב"א)

R. Yitzchak (d. 1210), often referred to as the Ritzva (ריצב"א = ר' יצחק בן אברהם), assumed leadership of the academy in Dampierre after the death of Ri.[71] He studied under Rabbenu Tam, but Ri was his primary teacher. The Ritzva is generally known as a *posek*, but he also appears in the printed *Tosafos* in at least seven tractates.

---

[70] The printed *Tosafos* on *Zevachim* is either *Tosafos R. Baruch* or heavily based on it. R. Baruch seems to have written a commentary on tractate *Tamid*, and may be the author of the commentary on *Sifra* attributed to R. Shimshon.

[71] The Ritzva is occasionally referred to as ריב"א. In such instances, it is easy to mistake the Ritzva for the early German Tosafist R. Yitzchak b. Asher HaLevi, also referred to as ריב"א in *Tosafos*. One prominent example of this is in tractate *Bava Kamma* 4b s.v. ועדים.

R. Shimshon b. Avraham of Shantz (ר״ש משאנץ/רשב״א)

R. Shimshon (d. 1214), known as the Rash MiShantz, or as the Rashba[72] (רשב״א = ר׳ שמשון בן אברהם) in the printed *Tosafos*, was the younger brother of the Ritzva, and was one of the most prolific *Ba'alei Tosafos*. In fact, the Rosh (*Teshuvos* 84:3) counts him along with Rabbenu Tam and Ri as the three pillars of the Tosafist movement. He was a student of Rabbenu Tam and R. Chaim Kohen, but his primary teacher was Ri. At the end of his life, he moved to Israel.[73]

R. Shimshon wrote *Tosafos Shantz* on the entire Talmud, although only a few tractates are extant. *Tosafos Shantz* is a record of the Ri's lectures with R. Shimshon's additions, featuring his own original insights. *Tosafos Shantz* were very influential and popular. The teachings of R. Shimshon appear often in the printed *Tosafos*, and many whole passages in our *Tosafos* are verbatim quotations from *Tosafos Shantz*.

R. Shimshon also wrote a *Mishna* commentary on *Sedarim Zeraim* and *Taharos* – printed as "פירוש הר״ש" alongside the Rambam in standard editions of the *Mishna*.[74]

---

[72] Not to be mistaken with R. Shlomo b. Aderes, the great Catalonian sage who flourished in the period of the later *Rishonim*.

[73] R. Avraham ben HaRambam writes how he and his father heard that R. Shimshon was in Akko but that they did not meet him as he did not pass through Egypt.

[74] R. Shimshon is attributed with a commentary on *Sifra*, but it is not clear if he is truly the author. R. Shimshon also wrote *Teshuvos*. Many of them were collected by his student R. Ya'akov b. Shlomo of

R. Yehuda of Paris (רבינו יהודה)

R. Yehuda (d. 1224) was one of Ri's last students. He is sometimes referred to as "רבינו האריה" or "Sir-Leon." R. Yehuda also studied under Ri's older students, such as R. Shimshon and R. Baruch. R. Yehuda's *beis midrash* was located in Paris.[75] R. Yehuda wrote a *Tosafos* commentary, *Tosafos Rabbenu Yehuda*, that were heavily based on the teachings of Ri.[76] We are only in possession of his *Tosafos* on tractate *Berachos*, but there are indications that he wrote on at least nineteen other tractates.[77]

Courson, and some are found in the *Or Zaruah, Sefer Mordechai*, and *Teshuvos Maimonios*. R. Shimshon also had a correspondence with R. Meir Abulafia (Ramah) regarding the Rambam's writings.

[75] There was a Torah center in Paris until 1182 when Philip Augustus expelled all of the Jews from the Parisian region (Ill-de-France). However in 1198, the expulsion was revoked and the Torah center re-emerged, ostensibly under R. Yehuda. Paris was an intellectual center in those days, even for Christian scholars, and it was called *Civitas Literarum*, קרית ספר, City of the Book.

[76] R. Yehuda quotes the Rambam in one place in his *Tosafos*, and this appears to be the first time one of the Tosafists quotes the Rambam in *Tosafos*, although we know from R. Shimshon's correspondence with the Ramah that he was aware of the writings of the Rambam. See also *Tosafos Yom Tov* on *Machshirin* 5:10.

[77] Other Students of Ri: (1) **R. Shimshon of Coucy** (שר מקוצי, d. 1221) wrote a *Tosafos* commentary and is also quoted occasionally in the printed *Tosafos*. Legend records that R. Shimshon was held captive for many years by a Muslim lord. Eventually, he escaped and saved the life of King Richard the Lionheart, who was lured into the lord's estate. Richard made him the Count of Coucy, and he served in this position for the remainder of his life. He was therefore known as the "Sar" of

The Talmudists of Germany

In Germany there were a number of great Talmudists who flourished during the period of the early *Rishonim*. They continued the German tradition, despite the destruction of the First Crusade that decimated much of the Rhineland communities.

R. Eliezer b. Nosson (ראב״ן)

R. Eliezer (d. 1170) lived in Mainz and served there as *Rosh Yeshiva*. He was a leader of the German Torah community during a time that France was emerging as the dominant Torah center under Rabbenu Tam. The Raavan was extremely well respected as a leading Talmudist and maintained a correspondence with his French contemporaries, most notably Rashbam and Rabbenu Tam. Many of his progeny, such as the Ravyah and Rosh, were great German rabbis and leaders in the subsequent generations.

Coucy. (2) **R. Yosef b. Baruch of Clisson** (d. 1221) is quoted in the printed *Tosafos*. He immigrated to Israel with R. Shimshon of Shantz in 1211, hence he is quoted occasionally as "R. Yosef Ish Yerushalayim." R. Yosef's route to Israel went via Egypt and R. Avraham b. HaRambam tells us "French scholars came to this land, the great Rabbi Yosef…" (*Milchamos Hashem* quoted in Urbach, *Ba'alei HaTosafot*, 319). So too, R. Yehuda AlCharizi visited Israel and wrote, "I met angels of God, pious Godly men, who came from France to dwell in Zion, and at their head is R. Yosef…" (ibid.).

The Raavan's major work was אבן העזר, (perhaps also known as צפנת פענח or פסקים של ראב״ן).[78] Much of the *sefer* is a collection of *minhagim* and local practices. Like many other works from Germany, his *sefer* sought to harmonize accepted practice with the *sugyos* in the Talmud.[79]

Chasidei Ashkenaz

At this time in Germany, there was also a group of pietists known as the *Chasidei Ashkenaz*. While the Talmudists we have been discussing were German *Ba'alei Tosafos* who followed in the way of Rashi, Rashbam, and Rabbenu Tam, the *Chasidei Ashkenaz* were connected to the old school of pre-crusade Germany. They focused more on straight explanations of the Talmud and less on the dialectics of the *Ba'alei Tosafos*. They were also heavily steeped in *sod* (mysticism) and wrote openly on *sod* topics.

---

[78] There is debate as to whether צפנת פענח was a separate *sefer* written by the Raavan or was one and the same with אבן העזר.

[79] The Raavan's Contemporaries: (1) **R. Yitzchak b. Mordechai** (Rivam, d. 1175) was a student of Riva and Rabbenu Tam. Rivam is quoted in the printed *Tosafos* on at least twelve tractates. He is not to be confused with R. Yitzchak b. Meir, a younger brother of Rabbenu Tam who is also referred to in *Tosafos* as Rivam. (2) **R. Ephraim b. Yitzchak** (Rabbenu Ephraim, d. 1175) of Regensburg was a major personality in Ashkenaz. He studied in France under Rabbenu Tam and maintained a correspondence with him upon returning to Germany. At various stages of his life he was involved in intense halachic controversy and debate. R. Ephraim is quoted in the printed *Tosafos* in over seven tractates (many times in *Chullin*). He also wrote at least one *sefer* (not extant) called ארבע פנים.

R. Shmuel b. Kalonymus (ר׳ שמואל החסיד, d. 1175) was one of the early *Rishonim* who was associated with this movement. R. Shmuel was a great-grandson of R. Eliezer HaGadol and was an important link in the German *sod* tradition. R. Shmuel lost his father when he was young, but his father entrusted the young Shmuel's caregiver with "*Tikun Tefilos*" and other mystical secrets. He commanded these secrets to be taught to Shmuel when the latter was older.

R. Shmuel served as *Rosh Yeshiva* in Speyer. There, he stressed learning areas of Torah that were not normally part of the general curriculum.[80] R. Shmuel also wrote commentaries on *midrashei halachah*, *agadah*, and *tefilah*. Even his Talmud commentary drew heavily on Torah verses, *midrashim*, and *Toras HaSod*. His writings were also filled with *gematrios*.

R. Shmuel's son, R. Yehuda HaChasid was also a major pietistic figure, and is attributed with the important work, *Sefer Chasidim*. His ethical and *halachic* will (*tzavah*) is also well known for its many original stringencies. A number of these stringencies have become incorporated into standard practice in some communities, such as the custom for a man not to marry a woman whose name is identical to that of his mother.

---

[80] See for example *Sefer Chasidim*, *siman* 1, regarding learning *Seder Kodashim*.

Students of the Raavan

After the Raavan, the Torah community in Germany was led by his sons-in-law and students.[81] Also at this time, R. Eliezer of Metz (author of *Sefer Yeraim*), one of Rabbenu Tam's foremost students, returned to Germany from his studies in France, and also served as a leader of the German Torah community.

R. Eliezer b. Yoel HaLevi (ראבי"ה)

R. Eliezer (d. 1225), also known as the Ravyah, was a grandson of the Raavan, and was a leading Talmud scholar in Germany.[82] His teachers included his grandfather (Raavan), his father (R. Yoel, son-in-law of Raavan), R. Eliezer of Metz, and R. Yehuda HaChasid.

The Ravyah wrote a number of important works. His most well-known is *Avi Ezri*, a *halachic* work that addresses laws that are applicable in contemporary times; therefore, the *sefer* focuses primarily on *Seder Mo'ed*, and tractates *Berachos* and *Chullin*. The *sefer* contains a nice amount of "*Tosafos*-style" teachings, includes important halachic *teshuvos*, and records many of the practices (*minhagim*) of

---

[81] The Raavan's sons-in-law were R. Shmuel b. Natronai (Rashbet) and R. Yoel. One of the Raavan's most central students was R. Moshe HaKohen, who is quoted a few times in the printed *Tosafos* and also studied under Rabbenu Tam.

[82] The Ravyah had a brother, R. Uri, who was burned *al kiddush Hashem* in 1216. A *kinah* about his death is published in *Gezerios Ashkenaz VeTzarfas*, 159.

Germany. The *Avi Ezri* is currently printed under the title *Sefer HaRavyah*.

The Ravyah also wrote a *sefer* called *Aviasaf* on *Sedarim Nashim* and *Nezikin*,[83] and a *Tosafos* style commentary on various tractates.

The Ravyah's Contemporaries

Some of the other major figures in Ashkenaz at this time were:

R. Simcha of Speyer (רבינו שמחה)

Rabbenu Simcha was one of the greatest figures of Germany. He was student of R. Eliezer of Metz and a colleague of the Ravyah. R. Simcha authored a halachic work called *Seder Olam*, which has been lost but is quoted by other *Rishonim*. R. Simcha also wrote a *Tosafos*-style Talmud commentary and important *teshuvos*.

R. Eleazar b. Yehuda of Worms (רוקח)

R. Eleazar (d. 1238) was a descendant of the famous Kalonymus family of Germany. He studied under R. Yehuda HaChasid and was associated with the *Chasidei Ashkenaz*. He was a prolific writer, especially in the area of ethics and

---

[83] The *Aviasaf* is quoted by other *Rishonim*, but is no longer extant. However, the 18th century Chida writes in his work *Shem Gedolim* (entry on the Ravyah) that he saw a copy of *Aviasaf* on *Nezikin*.

sod. Included among his dozens of works is an important halachic code called *Sefer Rokeach HaGadol*, a work on the laws and nature of repentance called *Moreh Chataim*, and a *Tosafos*-style Talmud commentary.[84]

---

[84] Another important contemporary of the Ravyah was **R. Baruch b. Shmuel** (ר׳ ברוך ממגנצא, d. 1221), who was a student of R. Eliezer of Metz and R. Moshe HaKohen. He was a leading German figure and author of a Talmud commentary. R. Baruch also authored a work called *Sefer HaChochmah*, which is no longer extant.

Early Rishonim of Ashkenaz

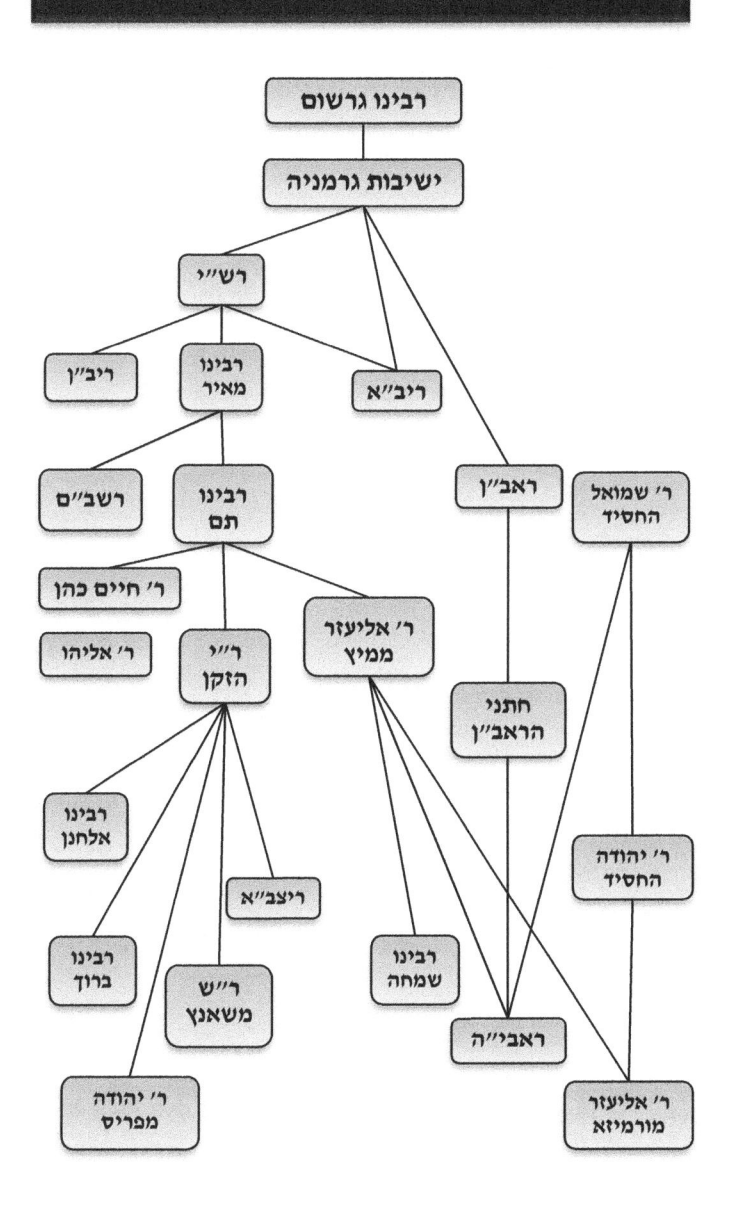

- רבינו גרשום
  - ישיבות גרמניה
    - רש"י
      - ריב"ן
      - רבינו מאיר
        - רשב"ם
        - רבינו תם
          - ר' חיים כהן
          - ר' אליהו
          - ר"י הזקן
            - רבינו אלחנן
            - רבינו ברוך
            - ר"ש משאנץ
              - ר' יהודה מפריס
            - ריצב"א
          - ר' אליעזר ממיץ
      - ריב"א
    - ראב"ן
      - חתני הראב"ן
        - ראבי"ה
      - רבינו שמחה
    - ר' שמואל החסיד
      - ר' יהודה החסיד
        - ר' אליעזר מורמיזא

THE EARLY RISHONIM OF PROVENCE

THE REGION OF PROVENCE IN southeastern France was situated between the Ashkenaz community of northern France and Germany and the Sephardic community of Spain and North Africa. Politically and socially, Provence (and the neighboring region on Languedoc) was more connected to Ashkenaz than it was to Spain. However, due to its proximity to Spain, the Provencal *Rishonim* were also exposed to, and influenced by, the Sephardic Torah culture.

The Torah center in Provence predates the period of the *Rishonim*. During the tenure of the *Geonim*, the city of Narbonne was an important Torah center in Provence. R. Moshe HaDarshan was one of the great scholar who flourished in 11th century Narbonne. Sources indicate that both his father and grandfather were heads of the *yeshiva* in Narbonne before him. One of R. Moshe's students was R. Nosson of Rome (d. 1106), author of the *Sefer HaAruch*, a Talmudic dictionary quoted often by the *Rishonim*.

Another important early figure in Narbonne was R. Yosef Tov Elem (d. 1050). Rav Yosef was a brother-in-law of R. Hai Gaon, and his commentary on Talmud and his *halachic* rulings are quoted by the *Rishonim*. Rav Yosef was also a *paytan* of note, and authored the concluding *piyut* of the Pesach Seder, "Chasal Siddur Pesach."

The Torah Community of Catalonia

Neighboring Provence to the south was Catalonia, a region that lies in northeastern Spain. The Torah community in Catalonia, became extremely influential during the period of the later *Rishonim* (ex. Rabbenu Yonah, Ramban, Rashba) with the cities of Barcelona and Gerona functioning as the major Torah centers. However, during the period of the early *Rishonim* we do not hear much of the Catalonian scholars. One of the few well-known early figures of Catalonia was R. Yehuda b. Barzilai of Barcelona (ר״י אברגלוני, d. early 1100's). He lived in Barcelona and his teachings were very influential in nearby Provence. He wrote a Talmud commentary on at least a few tractates, but none of it is extant. His major work was a *halachic* code, called *Sefer HaIttim*, which deals with the laws of the festivals. It draws from the teachings of R. Shmuel HaNagid and the *teshuvos* of Rif. It was a very important work before the appearance of the codes of the Rambam and Rosh. An earlier contemporary of his was R. Yitzchak of Barcelona, also called הרב מברגלוני. R. Yitzchak was also born in Barcelona but later moved to lead the community of Denia in Muslim Spain.

General Historical Overview

Provence was mostly under Christian control throughout the Middle Ages. The 10th century brought Muslim raiders to Provence, but, from the early 11th century through the mid-13th century, Provence was a fiefdom of the Holy Roman Empire. During much of that time period (starting in the early 12th century) Provence was directly ruled by the Christian Catalan (Catalonian) Dynasty. However, there were a number of local power struggles that led to unrest and shifts of power.

R. Avraham B. Yitzchak (רב אב ב"ד)

R. Avraham b. Yitzchak (d. 1159) was a prominent member of the Narbonne *Beis Midrash*,[85] and is often referred to as the "Rav Av Beis Din."[86] He was a student of R. Yehuda of Barcelona in neighboring Catalonia.

---

[85] **Narbonne Beis Midrash** – R. Avraham was a member of the Narbonne *Beis Midrash*, which for years was a major center of learning. An older contemporary and teacher of R. Avraham was **R. Moshe b. Yosef (Mirvan) of Narbonne (d. mid 1100's)**, *Rosh Yeshiva* in Narbonne. R. Moshe's uncle was R. Yitzchak b. Mirvan, a leading Rabbi in Narbonne in the early 12th century. R Moshe's grandfather, and R. Yitzchak's father, was R. Mirvan HaLevi, a prominent Jew in 11th century Narbonne.

[86] Hence he is also referred to as רי"א ב"ד, which is an acronym for רב אב בית דין. Rav Avraham is traditionally referred to as Raavad II, and is often time confused with his son-in-law, the prolific Raavad III who authored *hasagos* on the Rambam and wrote many halachic works.

R. Avraham wrote a commentary on the Talmud that has mostly been lost (except tractate *Bava Basra*). His major work that is extant is *Sefer HaEshkol*, a *sefer* of *pesakim*. The *sefer* has been printed in two very different editions.

R. Zerachiah HaLevi (בעל המאור/רז"ה)

R. Zerachiah (d. 1186) was born in Gerona, Catalonia and moved in his youth to Narbonne, Provence. There, he studied under Rav Avraham the "Rav Av Beis Din" and R. Moshe b. Yosef, Narbonne's *Rosh Yeshiva*. In 1145, R. Zerachiah moved to the Provencal city of Lunel as part of a migration of Rabbis from Narbonne to Lunel.[87]

R. Zerachiah's major work on Talmud was his *Sefer Maor*, authored by him at a very young age. This work gained for R. Zerachiah the title, "*Ba'al HaMeor*." The *Sefer Maor* contains the *Maor HaKatan*, authored on less complicated tractates that need "less light" to illuminate them, and the *Maor HaGadol* on tractates that need more elucidation. At its core, the *Sefer Maor* is a critique of Rif's *Halachos*. R. Zerachiah wrote tersely, and his style bears resemblance to that of the

---

Raavad I is the early Sephardic scholar, R. Avraham ibn Daud, author of *Sefer HaKabbalah*.

[87] **Beis Midrash of Lunel:** Lunel had an established Torah center. During the time period of the Rav Av Beis Din in Narbonne, the Torah center in Lunel was headed by **R. Meshulum of Lunel (d. 1170)**, author of the *Menorah Tehorah*.

early *Ba'alei Tosafos*, most notably Rabbenu Tam, who was a few years older than R. Zerachiah.[88]

R. Zerachiah also wrote a work of *klalei haTalmud* and Talmudic methodology called the *Sefer HaTzavah*, in addition to a number of other important works. These include *Hilchos Shechitah*, glosses on Raavad's *perush* on *Kinim*, *Sela HaMachlokes* (glosses on Raavad's *perush* on *Nidah*), *teshuvos*, and *piyutim*.

R. Yitchak b. Abba Mari of Marseilles (בעל העיטור)

Not much is known about R. Yitchak's life (d. 1193). He maintained a correspondence with the Rav Av Beis Din and Rabbenu Tam. His major work was *Sefer Ittur Sofrim*, more commonly referred to as the *Sefer HaIttur*.

The *Sefer HaIttur* was a popular work in the time of the *Rishonim*. It drew from the teaching of Ri of Barcelona (the author of *Sefer HaIttim*) and from R. Ephraim, a student of Rif. Unfortunately, current editions of *Sefer HaIttur* are filled with errors. R. Yitchak also wrote *Meah She'arim*, which contains comments on tractates from *Seder Nashim* and *Seder Nezikin*, and is printed in standard editions of the Talmud.

---

[88] The Ramban wrote a critique of the *Sefer Maor*, called *Milchamos Hashem*, where he defends the Rif from the young R. Zerachiah. It is interesting to note that the *Sefer Maor* and *Milchamos* were not included in the standard printings of the Rif until the 18th century.

R. Avraham b. Dovid (ראב״ד)

R. Avraham (d. 1197) was known as Raavad. He studied in Lunel, but is associated with the neighboring town of Posquieres (known today as Vauvert). He was one the leading figures to emerge from the Torah community of Provence.[89] Raavad was the student and son-in-law of the "Rav Av Beis Din," but his primary teacher was R. Meshulum of Lunel, author of the *Menorah Tehorah*.

His learning style generally followed the approach of his father-in-law, which is more Sephardic in style, focusing on *peshat* related issues and *pesak*. This was distinct from the approach of his older contemporary, R. Zerachiah, who was influenced by the Tosafist style of learning. The differing approaches of Raavad and R. Zerachiah led to many heated debates between these two great Provencal scholars.

The Raavad was a prolific writer. His writings and commentaries are known for their profundity, creativity, and sharp language.[90] Raavad wrote a commentary on the Talmud that is quoted often by the *Rishonim* after him.[91] Today we only have his commentary on four tractates.

---

[89] The Raavad was also a celebrated kabbalist, as was his son, R. Yitzchak Sagi Nahor.

[90] It is interesting to note that Raavad is not quoted much in Provence. Primarily his comments on the Talmud were popularized by the Ramban's *Beis Midrash*, while his other opinions and *teshuvos* were popularized by the *Kol Bo* and R. Yerucham.

[91] Ramban and Rosh quote him often. In fact, Meiri calls him "*Gedolei HaMeforshim*."

Although he wrote extensively, Raavad is most famous for his critical notes (*hasagos*) on the Rambam's *Mishna Torah*.[92] Some of Raavad's other works include: *Hilchos Lulav, Hilchos Netilas Yadayim, Issur VeHeter LaRaavad, Ba'alei HaNefesh* on the laws of *Nidah, Kasuv Sham* on R. Zerachiah's writings, and *Teshuvos HaRaavad*, which is a collection of responsa from Raavad, Raavad's father, and other *Rishonim*. Raavad also wrote on many obscure areas of Torah, and he authored a commentary on tractates *Kinim* and *Eduyos* and on the halachic *Midrash Toras Kohanim*.

R. Yonason of Lunel (ר״י מלוניל)

R. Yonason (d. 1215) learned under R. Moshe b. Yosef, the *Rosh Yeshiva* in Narbonne, and he was also a student and contemporary of R. Zerachiah and Raavad. R. Yonasan communicated with both the Ashkenazic and Sephardic Torah worlds, and had correspondences with the Ri and the Rambam. R. Yonasan's major work, *Chiddushei Rabbenu*

---

[92] The *Hasagos* start with the letters א״א, which stands for אמר אברהם. This is because early printers did not have different fonts or letters sizes, and hence inserting these letters would indicate to the reader that it was the Raavad's words and not those of the Rambam. There were many other *hasagos* that were left out of the original printings of the Rambam. Some are recorded in the commentary of the *Migdal Oz*, and have been now been printed with the other *hasagos* of the Raavad. Many of these later *hasagos* have been prefaced with the words "*Kasuv HaRaavad*." There are still other *hasagos* that are found in the commentaries of the *Maggid Mishna* and *Kesef Mishna* but have not been included in the printed *hasagos* of the Raavad.

Yonasan, is structured as a commentary on the Rif's *Halachos*.[93]

---

[93] **R. Avraham b. Nosson HaYarchei:** R. Avraham (d. 1215) was a contemporary of R. Yonasan in Luniel. There he learned under the Raavad and R. Yitzchak b. Abba Mari of Marseille. R. Avraham travelled to many different regions, including Germany, England, France (where he learned under the Ri and R. Elchanan), and Spain (where he led the Toledo *Beis Din*. R. Avraham's major work was *Sefer HaManhig*. It documents many *halachos* and local customs from the many different lands that he visited. There are two editions of *Sefer HaManhig*. The standard edition was printed in the 16th century, but it has many errors. A new updated and corrected edition was printed by Mosad HaRav Kook.

Early Rishonim of Provence

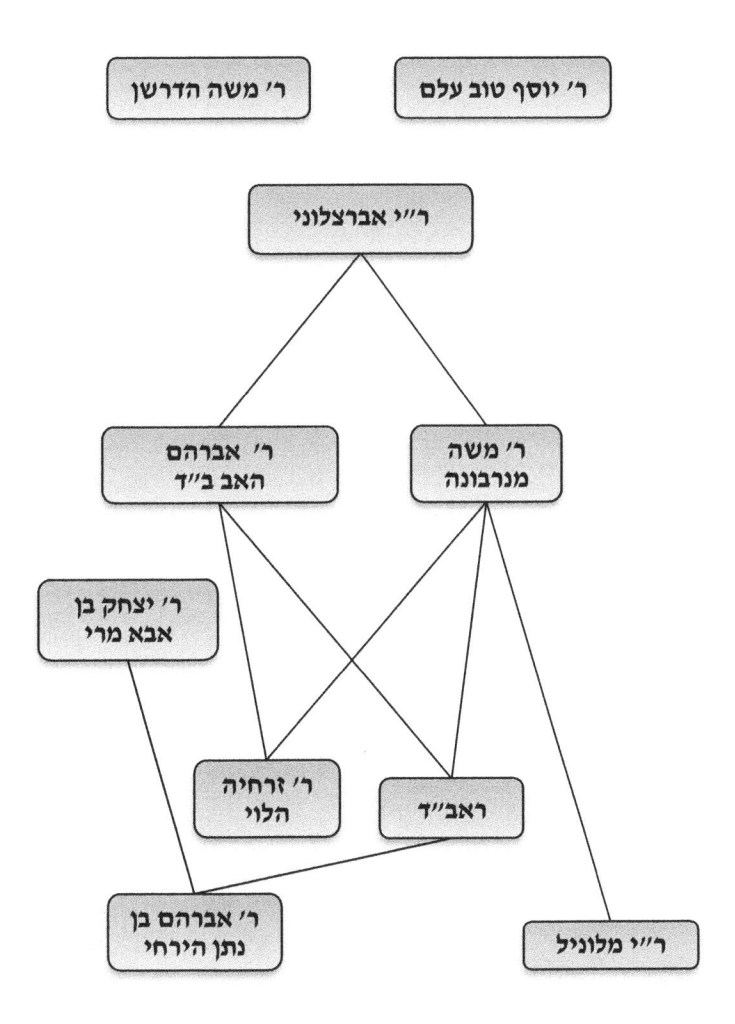

- ר' משה הדרשן
- ר' יוסף טוב עלם
- ר"י אברצלוני
- ר' אברהם האב ב"ד
- ר' משה מנרבונה
- ר' יצחק בן אבא מרי
- ר' זרחיה הלוי
- ראב"ד
- ר' אברהם בן נתן הירחי
- ר"י מלוניל

EPILOGUE

IN THESE PAGES, we have had the opportunity to discuss some of the more famous rabbinic figures who flourished during the period of the early *Rishonim*. We also explored the different geographic regions and schools of learning. However, there were hundreds of other rabbinic figures, their academies, and their students that we have not discussed. Indeed, many have been completely forgotten by history.

Looking back over the period, we notice the divergent histories of the Torah centers. During the period of the early *Rishonim* the North African Torah center reached great heights, but Muslim persecution drove its leaders to southern (Andalusian) Spain. Torah prospered there until the days of the Rambam, when the Andalusian Torah community also came to an end due to Muslim persecution. As we end the period of the early *Rishonim*, North Africa and Andalusian Spain are largely bereft of Torah learning.

Things were different, though, in Ashkenaz. Great Torah centers emerged and flourished in Germany and France. Major urban centers were home to great scholars, and illustrious *yeshivos* spotted the countryside. The crusades brought death and destruction to the cities of the Rhineland, but, amazingly, the German Torah community re-emerged from the darkness and Torah learning continued to prosper in Germany. As we end the period of the early *Rishonim*, Torah study is strong in Ashkenaz, and will continue that way for hundreds of years.

In Provence, Torah study was also consistently strong throughout the period of the early *Rishonim*. Moving forward to the period of the later *Rishonim*, Torah study would continue this way in Provence, but with a change in focus.

Made in United States
North Haven, CT
21 August 2022